MOTORSPORTS

Clive Gifford

WAYLAND

Published in 2012

Wayland
338 Euston Road
London NW1 3BH

Wayland Australia
Level 17/207 Kent Street
Sydney NSW 2000

Commissioning Editor: Jennifer Sanderson
Designer: Rob Walster, Big Blue
Illustrator: Ian Thompson
Picture Researcher: Clive Gifford
Proofreader: Katie Dicker

Picture Acknowledgements:
The author and publisher would like to thank the following agencies for allowing these pictures to be reproduced: cover, 34 Bertrand Guay/AFP; 3,28 Roslan Rahman/AFP; 5,32 AFP/AFP; 6 Jonathan Ferrey/Getty Images Sport; 7 Bob Martin/Sports Illustrated; 8, 9 AFP/AFP; 10 AFP/AFP; 11 Brian Cleary/Getty Images Sport; 12 George Tiedemann/Corbis;13 Aris Messinis/AFP; 15 Clive Mason/Getty Images Sport; 16 Stuart Franklin/Getty Images Sport; 17 x IStock; 17 IStock; 18 Damien Meyer/AFP; 19 AFP/AFP; 20 Chris McGrath/Getty Images Sport; 21 Kazuhiro Nogi/AFP; 22 Darrell Ingham/Getty Images Sport; 23 Mark Ralston/AFP; 24 Chris Trotman/Getty Images Sport; 25 Robert Cianflone/Getty Images Sport; 26 Javier Soriano/AFP; 27 Reporter Images/Getty Images Sport; 29 Doug Pensinger/Getty Images Sport; 30 Rusty Jarrett/Getty Images Sport; 31 Mark Thompson/Getty Images Sport; 33 Bryn Lennon/Getty Images Sport; 34 Kazuhiro Nogi/Getty Images Sport; 36 RacingOne/RacingOne; 37 Rusty Jarrett/Getty Images Sport; 38 Evaristo SA/AFP; 39 Marcel Mochet/AFP; 40 Jonathan Moore/Getty Images Sport; 41 Diego Tuson/AFP; 42 George Tiedemann/Sports Illustrated; 42 Jean-Loup Gautreau/AFP; 43 Grazia Neri/Getty Images Sport; 44 IStock

British Library Cataloguing in Publication Data
  Gifford, Clive
  Motorsports. - (Inside sport)
  1. Motorsports - Juvenile literature
  I. Title
  796.7

ISBN: 978 0 7502 6951 3

Printed in China

Wayland is a division of Hachette Children's Books,
an Hachette UK company.
www.hachette.co.uk

First published in 2009 by Wayland

This paperback edition published in 2012 by Wayland

CONTENTS

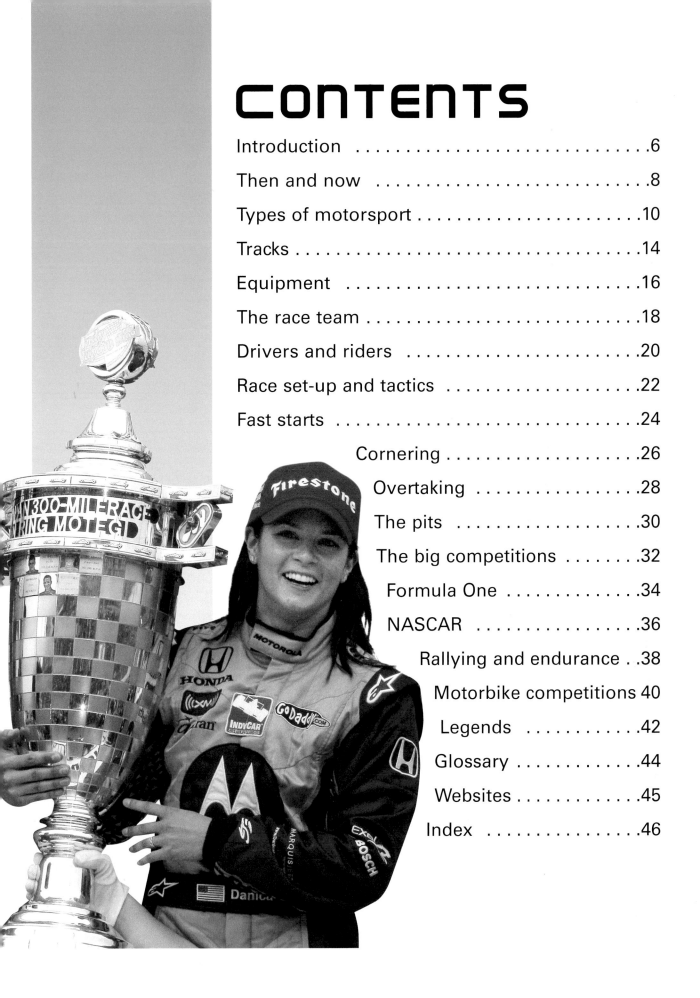

INTRODUCTION

Motorsports are competitions that allow people to pit their driving or riding skills, nerve, tactics and the technology they ride or drive on, against others.

Power and Speed

Modern racing cars and motorbikes have great power and speed. They are capable of rocket-like acceleration and incredible top speeds. A NASCAR racing at its top speed, for example, reaches about 320 km/h – it covers the length of a football field every second. Motorsport competitors need great physical and mental fitness and quick reactions to be able to handle these speeds. They also have to deal with powerful gravitational forces (or g-forces) when they enter turns at high speeds. They also need tremendous skill, courage and knowledge about their vehicle, their opponents and the track or route on which they are racing.

Drag racing pits two vehicles on a drag strip against each other. Here, John Force, winner of 10 National Hot Rod Association championships in a row, races. Force has reached speeds of more than 530 km/h.

Two racers compete in the 2008 Ice Speedway World Championship. Their bikes feature spikes to get a good grip on the icy surface.

Speed and Endurance

Motorsport competitions vary hugely. Most early racing was on open roads, but this is rare today. Instead, drivers race around dedicated circuits with cars, trucks, motorbikes or even school buses hurtling around the track for a set number of laps, trying to cross the finish line first.

A variation on this is endurance racing, where vehicles lap the track but try to complete as many laps and as great a distance as possible in a set amount of time, from hour-long trials to prestigious endurance events such as the 24 Hours of Le Mans race. Some racing is between small numbers of vehicles, such as pairs of dragsters or four motorcycle speedway riders hurtling around a small oval dirt track.

STAT ATTACK

High Attendances

400,000	Indianapolis 500 (2008)
332,000	Canadian Formula One Grand Prix (2006)
250,952	24 Hours of Le Mans (2007)
241,975	Spanish MotoGP (2006)
170,000	Final Champ Car race, California, United States (2006)
80,000	World Superbike weekend, the Netherlands (2005)

Fan-Tastic

While only a handful of people can drive or ride at the highest levels, millions of fans turn out to watch them. Throughout a World Rally Championship season, for example, more than 8 million people view the action. This is only the start, with tens of millions more watching the drama on television and the Internet. Many fans also enjoy motorsports at a lower level, watching local rallies and vintage cars from long ago in action.

THEN AND NOW

In 1895, the first edition of *The Autocar* magazine was published in Britain. The magazine assured readers that the car would never replace the horse, but it was wrong. Since then, millions of cars and motorbikes have been built and motorsports have developed into a popular pastime.

Early Racing

The earliest races tested vehicles' reliability and were often from one city to another. For example, the Paris-Bordeaux-Paris race was first held in 1895 and took more than 48 hours to complete. These early races took place along rutted tracks and roads, with drivers not wearing helmets. Often the cars or motorbikes did not have brakes. The first major race in the United States, the Vanderbilt Cup, took place in 1904 and in 1911, the first Indianapolis 500 (or Indy 500) took place.

The 1894 Paris to Rouen race was won at an average speed of 16.4 km/h. After that, racing car design moved on so quickly that by 1913, Percy Lambert averaged 160 km/h when racing for 60 minutes at the Brooklands circuit in England.

The 1930s and 1950s

The decades either side of the Second World War were important for motorsports with many advances, including the German Silver Arrow cars that were beautiful and fast.

The great Argentinean driver, Juan Manuel Fangio crosses the line to win his home Grand Prix. Fangio won five World Championships in four different makes of car in the 1950s.

Grand Prix races (meaning great prize), were run throughout Europe. The 1933 Monaco Grand Prix was the first to feature a starting grid based on qualifying times rather than on luck of the draw. The following year, there were a record 18 Grand Prix races; seven years earlier there had been only five. In the United States, racing around oval circuits, sometimes made of wooden boards, boomed while production cars raced on Daytona Beach in Florida – a forerunner of NASCAR (see page 12).

Major changes in motorsports occurred after the Second World War. The organisations that now run NASCAR, Formula One and Grand Prix motorcycling were all formed between 1945 and 1955. But despite advances, safety was still not a priority. One of the worst accidents in motorsports took place at the 1955 Le Mans race. Driver Pierre Levegh and more than 80 spectators were killed. Over time, new innovations in the design of vehicles, safetywear and track design have made motorsports safer without removing the risks involved.

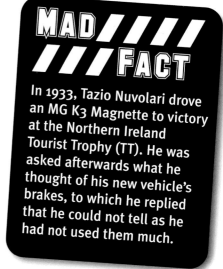

MAD FACT

In 1933, Tazio Nuvolari drove an MG K3 Magnette to victory at the Northern Ireland Tourist Trophy (TT). He was asked afterwards what he thought of his new vehicle's brakes, to which he replied that he could not tell as he had not used them much.

Michael Schumacher in a Ferrari wins the 2002 San Marino Grand Prix. Later that year he would capture the fifth of his seven World Championships, an astonishing feat.

TYPES OF MOTORSPORT

The many different types of motorsport are often known as classes and consist of racing on tracks, roads, over rough terrain and ice. The vehicles vary, from powerful single-seat cars to motorbikes and three-wheeled motorcycle sidecars.

Starting with Karting

Many famous motorsport stars, from Michael Schumacher and Jeff Gordon to Lewis Hamilton, had their first taste of racing in motorised karts. Karting is far from cheap but it is one of the most affordable types of motorsport. Its close racing on twisting tracks provides a good introduction to other classes. However, some racers stick to karting, the top competitors participating in the World and European championships. The top classes of kart can achieve speeds of up to 150 km/h and superkarts equipped with more powerful engines, can clock over 200 km/h.

Samin Gomez leads the pack in a karting race at the Le Mans race track. The young Venezuelan hopes to reach Formula One in the future.

Open-Wheel Racing

Single-seat cars specially built and prepared for racing on tracks are called open-wheel cars. They are different from regular vehicles because their wheels stick out from outside their narrow bodies. They also have a small cockpit in which the driver squeezes in feet first. The vehicles are lightweight but fitted with powerful engines. As a result, the top classes of open-wheel racing, such as IndyCar and Formula One, achieve very fast speeds. Paul Tracy in an IndyCar reached 413.5 km/h at the Michigan International Speedway in 1996, while at Monza in Italy, Formula One cars can reach 360 km/h.

Many open-wheel racing classes, such as the Toyota Atlantic Championship and Formula Three, act as feeder competitions to bigger classes. Others are run as steps up into single-seater racing after a driver has built experience in karting. These include Formula Ford, Formula Vee and A1GP. Starting in 2005, A1GP is unusual in that teams race under national colours with identical engines and bodies. Although slower than Formula One cars, the cars drive closer together over shorter races.

MAD FACT

In 1990, A.J Foyt's IndyCar's brakes failed at the Road America circuit sending him hurtling down the track at almost 300 km/h. The crash shattered his legs but the following year, he qualified for the Indy 500 at the age of 56.

Touring and Stock Cars

Touring cars are race-modified versions of standard cars. They are fitted with high-performance engines, brakes, suspension and have added safety features. Sometimes, a frame inside the car, called a roll cage, is fitted to protect drivers should their vehicle overturn. Although touring cars do not travel quite as fast as many open-wheel classes, the racing is intense with frequent overtaking and the lead changing many times in a race.

Stock cars are also raced on tracks over a series of races, with points awarded for position. They were originally so-called because the cars were 'in stock' at a car dealer's and available for sale to the public. However, over time, the most famous stock car competitions, such as the National Association for Stock Car Auto Racing (NASCAR), feature cars and trucks that are purpose-built for racing.

Rallying

Rally drivers race over roads, tracks and countryside against the clock. Rallies are split up into a number of timed individual stages. Drivers do not race directly against their rivals –

STAT ATTACK

World Rally Championship Facts

Most championships: Eight, Sébastien Loeb (2004–2011)

Fastest rally: 122.86 km/h average speed, 2005 Rally of Finland

Smallest margin of victory: 0.2 seconds, 2011 Jordan Rally won by Sebastien Ogier

instead they set off at regular intervals and look to complete a stage consisting of different types of terrain and conditions in the quickest possible time. Often, in each car, a co-driver, who navigates with split-second precision, sits alongside the driver.

Motorcycle Motorsports

Motorcycle racing is incredibly popular at both amateur and professional levels. Many amateur riders enjoy motocross racing all-terrain motorbikes around a closed-off dirt circuit with humps and dips. At the top level, motocross and supercross (which features shorter courses than motocross) see spectacular racing. In the hugely popular Speedway events, four riders power and slide their way around a small oval dirt track on bikes that do not have brakes. Motorbikes, usually grouped by the size and power of their engine, are also raced on hard road circuits. At one end of the scale are tiny pocket bikes that generate only one-eighth of the power of a normal family car, while at the other end are powerful beasts like MotoGP and Superbikes with 800 to 1,000cc engines capable of top speeds of 320 km/h.

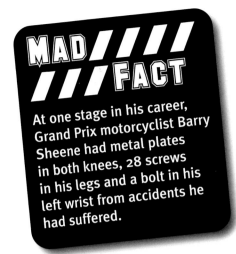

MAD FACT

At one stage in his career, Grand Prix motorcyclist Barry Sheene had metal plates in both knees, 28 screws in his legs and a bolt in his left wrist from accidents he had suffered.

Motorcycle mayhem is guaranteed in a Supercross race. Supercross races are over dirt courses held inside an arena or stadium. With tight turns, hills, jumps and ditches, they promise exciting racing for spectators.

# TRACKS

While rallying and some other events take place across rough terrain or on roads, most modern motorsports are held on tracks or circuits. Many of these have unique characteristics that place particular demands on a driver or rider and their race vehicle.

Types of Track

Many of the tracks used, such as Indianapolis, are oval-shaped with the turns banked or angled. The banking allows the cars to maintain high speeds as they corner. Some tracks are tri-ovals with three long straights and three sets of turns. NASCAR racing favours oval tracks but races occasionally take place on road or street circuits that contain lots of different twists and turns. Road or street circuits are used by Formula One, A1GP, touring cars and many forms of motorcycle racing including MotoGP. Most tracks have a smooth asphalt surface but those used in motorcycle Speedway are dirt-covered. Motocross courses are full of humps, hills, jumps and ditches.

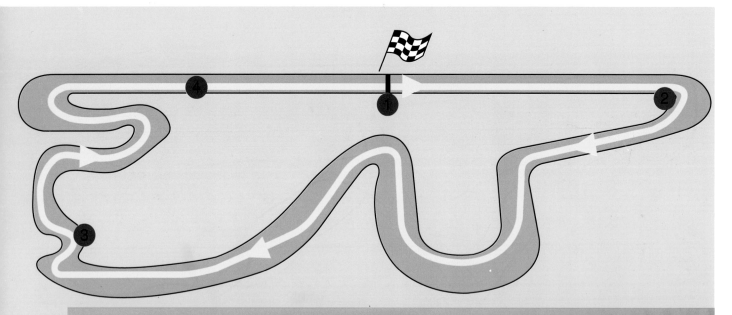

This is a diagram of a typical circuit used for track racing competitions such as MotoGP motorbikes and touring cars. The yellow line shows a good racing line around the track.

1. *Start/finish line*
2. *Hairpin bend*
3. *S-shaped turns, often known as esses*
4. *Straight where vehicles reach top speeds*

Track Features

Races on nearly all tracks begin with the cars or bikes lining up on the starting grid, a marked-out area on the track, with each vehicle having a specified place to start. The start-finish line is where every lap is completed. On road circuits there are a variety of bends. A hairpin bend is a tight 180 degree turn that vehicles have to take very slowly. A chicane is usually a pair of small bends, one to the left and one to the right. At many turns, there are run-off areas that allow a driver or rider to stay safe even if he or she misses the turn, while tyre walls and various forms of safety barriers line a circuit. There is usually a pit lane that links the track to the pit area where teams can re-fuel and repair race vehicles.

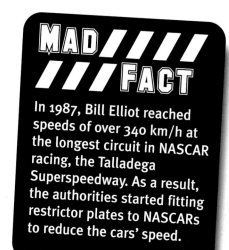

MAD FACT

In 1987, Bill Elliot reached speeds of over 340 km/h at the longest circuit in NASCAR racing, the Talladega Superspeedway. As a result, the authorities started fitting restrictor plates to NASCARs to reduce the cars' speed.

Famous Circuits

Each track has its own unique design, atmosphere and may favour a particular type of vehicle or driver. For example, most Formula One tracks run clockwise but the Interlagos track in Brazil runs anti-clockwise, putting drivers under real pressure. Most tracks are built on the outskirts of a city but Monaco remains an exception. First run in 1929, the circuit runs through the streets of the principality of Monte Carlo, giving few chances for overtaking but offering thrilling close-up views for spectators. Of the oval tracks, the 4.02 kilometre-long Indianapolis Motor Speedway is the most famous and one of the oldest circuits in the United States.

Lewis Hamilton in his McLaren on the way to victory at the 2008 Monaco Grand Prix. McLaren with 15 victories on the famous 3.34 km-long street circuit, has been the race's most successful team.

EQUIPMENT

Great riders and drivers need equally great machines to propel them to victory. Their cars and motorcycles must be fast, stable and reliable. They should handle well and hold together under the severe forces a rider or driver puts them through.

From Computer to Victory

Most race vehicles begin life on computer workstations. These are equipped with design, testing and engineering software so that designers and technicians can experiment with computer simulations to see how the cars or bikes might fair. Once the vehicle is built, it undergoes hundreds of hours of testing on closed tracks. The role of a test driver is vital. He or she reports back on the performance and handling of the vehicle. Data about the engine, brakes, tyres and other crucial components are sent back to computers by radio signals for team engineers to analyse. For many classes of motorsport, the process of improvement never stops.

MAD FACT

A 1966-Chevrolet Chevelle was so fast in a NASCAR race that officials were suspicious. It turned out that the vehicle, built by Henry 'Smokey' Yunick, was a seven-eighths-scale model of a full size car.

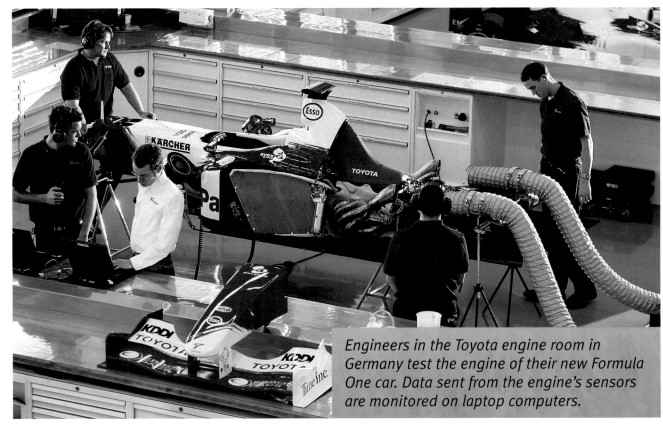

Engineers in the Toyota engine room in Germany test the engine of their new Formula One car. Data sent from the engine's sensors are monitored on laptop computers.

Throughout the race season, teams try to find ways to make improvements to their vehicles. What may seem like minor improvements, can slice a tiny amount off a lap time that, over the many laps of a race, can be the difference between first and second place on the podium.

Wings and Things

Since the 1920s, designers have tried to build vehicles that are increasingly aerodynamic and streamlined. This helps to reduce drag (the friction from the air as the vehicle races by) and means that the vehicle can go faster or use less power and fuel to maintain the same speed as a less-streamlined vehicle. For example, a MotoGP motorbike has a sculpted fairing in front of the rider to help channel the airflow smoothly around the bike. Many racing cars feature wings or spoilers, which are shaped like upside-down wings, to generate downforce (the opposite of lift). Downforce helps 'glue' a car to the ground by giving it more grip. However, it comes at the cost of creating more drag, so designers and engineers aim to balance the two forces.

A mechanic removes an electric blanket from a race tyre. Blankets are used to keep a tyre at the ideal temperature before it is fitted to the vehicle.

Under Scrutiny

All motorsports have strict rules and regulations about vehicles' size, weight, features and engine design and power. Teams have to follow these rules or face a hefty fine, losing points in a competition or being disqualified completely. The rules are strict. For example, in a 2007 NASCAR race, Brian Vicker's car was disqualified for being 4 millimetres too low. In many disciplines of motorsport, there are weight restrictions on vehicles because the lighter the vehicle, the quicker its engine can power it. Teams have been known to race underweight and then try to add weight to the vehicle when it is weighed after the race. Race stewards are officials whose job is to uncover accidental or deliberate rule-breaking.

Disc brakes on racing cars are powerful and expensive. They have to stop a Formula One car travelling at 300 km/h to a standstill in just 4 seconds. The brakes can reach temperatures of up to 1,000 degrees Celsius.

THE RACE TEAM

Race teams consist of many people working together to give their drivers or riders every possible chance of success. The top levels of motorsports are incredibly expensive to enter so teams have to find ways of bringing in finance to keep them racing.

The support team around a race car and driver can be seen from this photograph of the Mitsubishi team vehicles setting up base in Mali during the 2006 Dakar Rally. Trucks carry supplies, spare parts and key personnel between the rally's stages.

The Costs of Racing

In the past, many amateurs entered events using their own money or money from well-wishers. Today, running a competitive racing team in a major motorsports competition costs a lot of money. In NASCAR, it can be upwards of £12 million per car and many times that in Formula One. How do these sums mount up? The driver, mechanics and other staff salaries can be a major part of the total but it is also the cost of the parts used in racing that push up the final bill. For example, a NASCAR team spends approximately £10,000 a race on tyres, while a Formula One car engine costs over £100,000 and is used for just two races in a row.

Sponsors and Revenue

Some race teams are bankrolled by major car manufacturers such as the Citroën Total World Rally Championship team. Most however, rely on gaining finance from race winnings, merchandise sales, television rights and most importantly, sponsorship. In Formula One, sponsorship can make up more than 80 per cent of a team's revenue.

The biggest sponsor of a race team is called the primary sponsor and may have control of the vehicle's colour scheme and name. Co-sponsors and trade link-ups are lesser sponsors who either supply free equipment or travel, or pay smaller sums to be linked to a team. In the past, many race teams were sponsored by tobacco companies but this has since been banned in many countries and competitions.

Team Bosses

The team boss or principal is the head of a racing team. He or she has the unenviable job of finding sponsors and keeping them happy, as well as running a competitive, well-performing, race team. Some of the most successful team bosses, including NASCAR's Jack Rousch, Frank Williams and Ron Dennis in Formula One, and Davide Tardozzi in World Superbikes, are expertly skilled at negotiations and spotting talented drivers, engineers and support staff.

2008 Formula One World Champion Lewis Hamilton and McLaren team boss, Ron Dennis are all smiles following a successful practise session at the 2008 Turkish Grand Prix.

DRIVERS AND RIDERS

Top motorsport drivers and riders appear to have a glamorous life. They get to drive or ride the world's fastest race vehicles, are adored by fans and are well-rewarded financially. But behind the glitz and fame, lies mountains of hard work, dedication and risk.

The Demands of Racing

For drivers and riders, the hard work starts a long way away from the race as they and their team test and improve their vehicle. They work with their team to develop tactics, meet sponsors and fulfill media commitments. Whether they want to talk or not, drivers and riders are usually under contract to attend press conferences and give interviews. The clamour for autographs and time with fans can also be intense.

The physical and mental stresses and strains on a top driver or rider can be phenomenal. They must be physically and mentally fit to cope with race conditions. Strong gravitational forces pull and push drivers or riders as they enter and exit turns. Their fireproof clothing adds to car temperatures of 45–50 degrees Celsius to make conditions unbearable. Even if the weather at the race track is not particularly warm, racers can lose three kilograms of body weight in a race. Most of this is perspiration, so many helmets come with a built-in water or sports drink supply. Drivers and riders train to build strength in their leg, arm and neck muscles and to increase their stamina so that they can withstand the rigours of racing.

Australian IndyCar driver, Ryan Briscoe celebrates after winning the Honda Indy 200 in 2008. The race took just over two hours to complete.

Racing Safely

Safety has increased greatly since the daredevil days of early racing. Today, drivers and riders wear hi-tech clothing with fireproof layers capable of withstanding heat of more than 600 degrees Celsius. Safety features in cars include removable steering wheels that allow drivers to get out of crashed cars more quickly.

Tragically, accidents and deaths still occur in all motorsports. In 2011, Indy Car Series champion, Dan Wheldon and Marco Simoncelli, MotoGP racer both died after racing accidents. All drivers and riders know that each time they head out to race, a risk of injury or death still remains.

Mattia Pasini loses control of his 125cc motorcycle during the Japanese Grand Prix in 2004. The Italian came off his bike at high speed but his helmet and racewear enabled him to walk away from the accident without serious injury.

21

RACE SET-UP AND TACTICS

Teams adjust their race vehicles to perform at their best on a particular route or circuit. The precise way a vehicle has its engine, brakes, suspension and other parts selected and tuned for a particular race, is known as the set-up.

Set-Up and Handling

How a race vehicle handles around a circuit or part of a rally course is down to a combination of many factors. Although it starts with the vehicle's overall design, from race to race, elements of the handling can be adjusted by altering or adjusting parts such as the brakes, tyres and suspension. As the only point of contact between the whole machine and the track, tyres are especially crucial. Choosing slick or intermediate tyres, for example, can cost a driver the race if the weather suddenly turns. Although parts of the vehicle may be altered to reduce tyre wear, tyres may last just one race or even just part of a race.

Brazilian racer, Roberto Moreno looks on as his Patrick Racing team engineers make adjustments to his car's set-up at the Texas Motor Speedway. The smallest adjustments can be crucial to the team.

Performance Data

Throughout many forms of motorsport competitions, electronic sensors connected to a radio transmitter send large volumes of data about the vehicle, its parts and their performance back to the team base. This information is known as telemetry. Teams analyse the telemetry to assess the vehicle's performance and identify issues or potential problems – for example, a team may call a driver or rider into the pits earlier than planned to adjust or replace a part. In testing or practise before a race or competition, the telemetry as well as the driver's or rider's comments can play a huge part in determining the set-up of the vehicle on race day.

Race-Day Tactics

All drivers and riders want to go as fast as possible for as long as possible, but a team may develop more complex tactics to give itself the best chance of victory. This may involve the driver or rider coming in for pit stops at certain times or being told to push harder at one point or to run a little slower to save fuel or wear on the tyres, engine or other parts. Teams pay much attention to their race strategy but races are dynamic, and situations can change dramatically, forcing teams to revise their strategy as the race progresses.

Michael Schumacher celebrates a race win with one of his trademark celebratory jumps. In his career, Schumacher finished on the podium a staggering 154 times.

FAST STARTS

In the past, the 24 Hours of Le Mans race featured its own unique start, with drivers running to their cars, clambering in and firing up the engines. Today, Le Mans and most other motorsport events held on tracks feature a start with riders or drivers in or on their vehicles, engines running, waiting for the signal to start.

Under Starter's Orders

While rally drivers usually begin a stage on their own in timed intervals, most motorsports feature a massed start. This may be as little as four speedway riders starting in a straight line or more than 40 cars in NASCAR. The starting order is usually determined by qualifying times. The fastest lap time leads to a driver or rider starting from pole position (first) on the grid. The slower their qualifying time, the further back a driver or rider will start.

MAD //// //// FACT

From a standing start, a typical Formula One car can accelerate from 0-96 km/h in between 1.9 and 2.7 seconds. It can reach 240 km/h in as little as 5 seconds.

Some classes of motorsport, including IndyCar and NASCAR, use a rolling start where the cars move around the track in race order. Others, such as Formula One and MotoGP use a standing start with the vehicles waiting for the starting lights to go out before pulling away. Quick reactions and an awareness of other vehicles' positions are required at the start to steal any possible advantage in a race's early stages. Drivers and riders look for gaps to speed through while staying aware of others trying to overtake them.

Jeff Gordon in car 24 and Denny Hamlin in car 11 are at the front of the field for the start of the 2008 Goody's Cool Orange 500 at the Martinsville Speedway. All drivers are looking for the best possible start.

Acceleration

How quickly a vehicle can increase its speed at the start of a race and after travelling through a slow corner, is so important in all classes of motorsport. Racers want as much acceleration as possible but not so much that they lose control of their vehicle. Open-wheel cars, with their light weight and powerful engines, are amongst the quickest at acceleration. An IndyCar is capable of accelerating from 0–160 km/h in just three seconds. A Formula One car can reach the same speed in just over two seconds.

A crowded procession of V8 Supercars during a race. As they pull away from the start, drivers try to accelerate hard whilst staying aware of and avoiding the vehicles ahead of them. They stay on the lookout for opportunities to overtake.

STAT ATTACK

Le Mans endurance

The 24 Hours of Le Mans is a huge test of acceleration and reliability. The 2011 winning car, an Audi R18 TDI completed 355 laps of the Le Mans track – covering a staggering distance of 4839 km. That is further than from London to Moscow and back, all at an average speed of over 216 km/h.

Lasting the Distance

There is no value in having the fastest motorbike or car if it breaks down under the pressure of racing and does not complete the race or limps to the finishing line. Reliability is essential and one of the main reasons why race teams spend so much time, effort and money on testing. It is not just the whole vehicle that is put through its paces. Many of the most crucial components such as the engine, brakes and suspension are tested separately to try to make sure that they do not fail during competition.

CORNERING

Cornering is a major test of skill. Drivers and riders need tremendous levels of timing and sometimes, courage to approach the corner on the right line, brake at the last moment and time their exit.

Cornering

Cornering is an art and comes with much practise and experience. Throughout a race, drivers and riders are looking to take the racing line – the quickest, smoothest and most efficient route. Getting on the racing line for corners is especially important. Mistakes are most likely to be made in corners and this can result in losing valuable time, allowing a rival to overtake or the vehicle leaving the track and crashing out of the race. Entering a hairpin bend, for example, drivers aim to brake very hard and turn as late as possible to get on a racing line close to the inside of the bend. Before they have straightened their vehicle completely, they will be back down on their accelerator or throttle, looking to power out of the turn.

Corner Forces

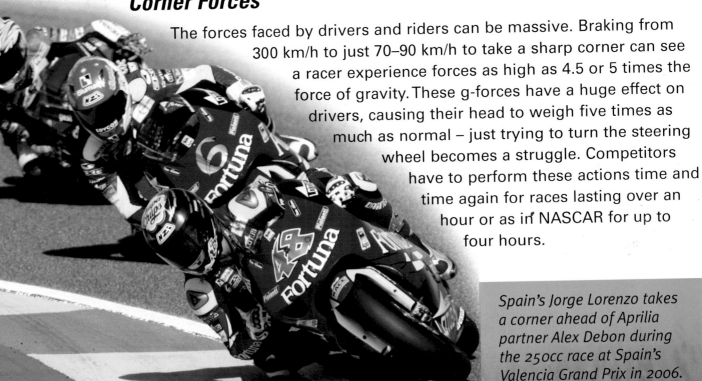

The forces faced by drivers and riders can be massive. Braking from 300 km/h to just 70–90 km/h to take a sharp corner can see a racer experience forces as high as 4.5 or 5 times the force of gravity. These g-forces have a huge effect on drivers, causing their head to weigh five times as much as normal – just trying to turn the steering wheel becomes a struggle. Competitors have to perform these actions time and time again for races lasting over an hour or as in NASCAR for up to four hours.

Spain's Jorge Lorenzo takes a corner ahead of Aprilia partner Alex Debon during the 250cc race at Spain's Valencia Grand Prix in 2006.

Different Techniques

Cornering techniques vary in different classes and under different race conditions. Track motorcyclists facing a tight corner shift their bodyweight and angle their bikes. Mere millimetres can exist between their knee and the track surface as they lean themselves and their bike sharply into hairpins and chicanes. This is why their race clothing includes a knee pad area called a slider. Motocross and speedway riders facing a flat corner on a dirt track often use their feet to slide the back of their bike around the curve. Rally drivers often use a similar technique, oversteering their car to let the back wheels slide sideways round the corner.

Sébastien Loeb uses a little bit of oversteer to let the rear end of his Citroën C4 slide round a corner at the 2007 World Rally Championship Rally of Norway.

OVERTAKING

Many motorsport races are decided by the ability of one driver or rider to overtake and pass others.

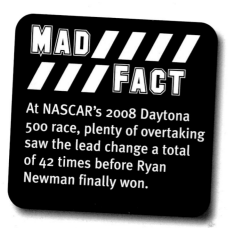

The Art of Overtaking

Overtaking is very dependent on the circuit, the type of race vehicles and the race conditions. Certain circuits have wide passing areas near corners or long straights that, if there is a big difference in speed between vehicles, faster drivers or riders can use to power past others. Other tracks, such as the Monaco Grand Prix circuit, are extremely tight and make overtaking very difficult. Oval tracks such as those used in NASCAR and IndyCar races, are wide and often feature three or four vehicles racing abreast. Drivers look to nip ahead on the inside or power around the outside of an opponent. Rising up the banking means travelling a greater distance, so drivers need to rely on the speed of their cars to overtake successfully.

Australian MotoGP rider, Casey Stoner overtakes on the outside of rival Dani Pedrosa as the pair travels round a corner at the Sepang International Circuit.

Who is...

...Jimmie Johnson?

Johnson began racing 50cc motorcycles as a young child but later moved into four-wheeled racing, mainly in offroad competitions. His first NASCAR BUSCH Series race was in 1998. He became a full-time NASCAR driver in 2000 and moved up into NASCAR's elite series in 2002. In 2006, he led the field with 24 top-ten finishes and five race wins to become the Sprint Cup series champion. The following year, he defended the title with further wins in 2008, 2009 and 2010 to become the only drive in NASCAR history to win five consecutive championships.

Jimmie Johnson leads Jeff Gordon and Carl Edwards in the Allstate 400 race in 2008. Johnson won the race on his way to becoming NASCAR's Sprint Cup champion in 2008.

Cars racing on oval tracks, especially NASCARs, make much use of a technique called drafting. This is where one vehicle drives close behind a lead vehicle with the two effectively sharing the same pocket of air. The car behind can sometimes drop back a little further and then find itself sucked forward by air pressure, helping it to pull out and overtake. Some drivers and riders use outbraking to get past their rivals. They brake later than their rivals hoping to race ahead of their opponent around the corner. Another strategy is to fake an overtaking move on one side of a rival, only to swoop past on the other side.

Overtaking Aids

A novel feature of some racing classes, including Champ Cars in the past and A1GP racing today, is an overtake or powerboost button. This button, fitted to the driver's steering wheel, gives the car an extra dash of power (in CART cars, it was an additional 50 horsepower) to assist them with overtaking. It can be used only a set number of times, for example in A1GP, four times in the sprint race and eight times in the feature race (see pages 32–33).

THE PITS

Race mechanics and support staff watch the race from the pits. The pit crew waits for its drivers or riders to come in during the race for repairs, fuels or new tyres.

Pit-Stop Procedure

Many pit stops are planned in advance but drivers or riders who have a problem can inform their team by radio and come in for a pit stop. The vehicle exits the track via the pit lane, a road that takes it to the pit area, where the pit-stop team leaps into action. The team will have practised every scenario so that it can perform its job following the safety rules, but in the shortest amount of time. One or more members of the team might re-fuel the car, while mechanics work on each wheel, replacing tyres by removing and putting on a complete new wheel and tyre. Other pit-stop personnel may clean visors or windscreens. With the pit crew's work complete, the driver or rider is given a signal to leave the pit – in Formula One, this is the job of the lollipop man. For safety, there is a speed limit in the pit lane.

MAD //// //// FACT

At the 1979 Rebel 500 NASCAR race, top driver Dave Pearson came in for a pit stop. He pulled out before his crew had secured all the wheels and as he got to the end of the pit lane, both his left-side wheels fell off!

Quick Stops

The length of the stop is often determined by how much fuel needs to be added to the vehicle. Mistakes or the need to make repairs to the vehicle, can cost valuable seconds and race positions. Pit stops in Formula One can be less than six seconds long, in NASCAR less than

A gas man (left) refuels Bill Elliot's NASCAR with a 12 US gallon (45.4 litre) can. The man to his right holds a spare fuel can and catches any fuel overspill.

14 seconds, while the A1GP championship has an award for the team that makes the fastest stops over the season. Endurance racing has different pit stop rules from many other types of motorsport. The engine has to be switched off and re-fuelling and repairs have to be conducted separately. Often, drivers are also changed during a pit stop.

Pit-Stop Tactics

In some competitions, vehicles are forced to make a number of pit stops in a race. In others, it is up to the team to decide when it calls in its rider or driver. Much thought goes into the strategy because in pit stops, every second or fraction of a second counts. Sometimes, a team will leave its driver or rider out for a few more laps to build up an extra lead before coming into the pits. On other occasions, such as when the weather conditions change greatly, it may call the driver or rider in early to fit a different type of tyre.

Lewis Hamilton's pit team launches into action at the Malaysian Grand Prix. Three person mini-teams are situated at each wheel to change the vehicle's tyres in seconds. The lollipop man (top right) holds a sign in front of the driver and will turn it to let the driver know when he can pull away.

THE BIG COMPETITIONS

The most eagerly anticipated events of the motorsport year are the standout individual races and the big competitions on the calendar. These attract thousands of spectators who come to see the best drivers, riders and machines in action.

IndyCar Series

The premiere single-seat motorsport competition in North America, the IndyCar Series is run by the Indy Racing League (IRL). The 2008 season featured 18 points-scoring races and a demonstration race in Queensland, Australia. Most of the circuits are ovals although street circuits are raced in Edmonton (Canada), Long Beach (California) and on Japan's Twin Motegi circuit. Non-American drivers have found much success in the series, but the overall race-win record holder remains Sam Hornish Jr with 19 wins and three championship titles.

A1GP

Beginning in 2005, the A1GP offers spectators two races over a weekend – a short sprint race and a longer, feature race. The sprint race winner receives 10 points followed by 8, 6, 5, 4, 3, 2 and 1 for the next seven finishers. In the feature race, each car has to make two pit stops and the race winner receives 15 points. The next three placed cars receive 12, 10 and 8 points and then one less point per place so that tenth place receives one point. In addition, one extra point is awarded to the driver who makes the fastest lap. These points go to the national team not the driver, so drivers can be switched between races.

Danica Patrick poses with the trophy for winning the Indy Japan 300 in 2008. She finished sixth in the 2008 Championship – the highest-placed American driver.

Andy Priaulx powers through the wet during race 2 of the 2006 FIA World Touring Car Championship.

Teams for the 2008–09 season include Korea for the first time joining a strong Asian contingent that includes Malaysia, India and Pakistan as well as many teams from Europe, the Americas and elsewhere.

STAT ATTACK

A1GP Top Nations

Year	First	Second	Third
2007-08	Switzerland	New Zealand	Great Britain
2006-07	Germany	New Zealand	Great Britain
2005-06	France	Switzerland	Great Britain

World Touring Car Championship

There have been numerous competitions for touring cars and one World Championship for them held in 1987. Since 2005, a World Touring Car Championship has been held. Pairs of races are held at either 11 or 12 different tracks in a season with the top eight finishers receiving points. Consistency and staying in the points is crucial. In the 2007 championship, Swiss driver Alain Menu won five of the 22 races held but lost the championship to Andy Priaulx because he had more higher-placed finishes.

FORMULA ONE

Considered by many to be the ultimate motorsport competition, Formula One is certainly the most followed and the most expensive for teams to take part in.

Globetrotters

Formula One is a global motorsport with races on almost every continent. The 2008 season featured 18 races, beginning in Australia and ending in Brazil. Teams travel about 160,000 kilometres a year between their headquarters in Europe, test facilities and the varying race circuits. The Formula One team is a huge operation with tonnes of equipment as well as usually three cars and dozens of staff, which are transported all over the world.

The 2006 World Champion, Fernando Alonso leads 2007 World Champion, Kimi Räikkönen during the 2008 Hungarian Grand Prix. The race winner, Heikki Kovalainen, completed the 306.6-km course in 97 minutes 27.1 seconds, an average speed of over 220 km/h.

State of the Art

A Formula One car is a highly-advanced machine made using state of the art materials and technology. The vehicles are light in weight. They weigh just 600 kilograms, including the driver, and feature engines that run at speeds three to four times that of an ordinary family car. Everything about a Formula One car is high performance, from the electronic steering wheels with gear changers to disc brakes that reach temperatures above 1,000 degrees Celsius and can slow the car from 290 km/h to 90 km/h in under two seconds. Top teams spend millions on testing and refining their cars before and during the race season.

The Grand Prix Weekend

A race weekend starts with free practises at the circuit on Friday and qualifying for the race on Saturday. There are three separate short qualifying periods. The slowest cars are then prevented from taking part in the next qualifying session. The final qualifying session is just ten minutes long but determines tenth place to pole position on the starting grid. With some tracks difficult to overtake on, being on the front row of the grid is vital.

Lewis Hamilton fights to regain control of his McLaren after colliding with his close rival Felipe Massa at the 2008 Japanese Grand Prix. Although Hamilton finished 12th in this race, he became the youngest driver to win the World Championship.

Each Formula One race is about 305 kilometres long and lasts approximately 90 minutes. Races are often packed with drama and incidents. The race winner receives 10 points, the runner-up 8 and then the next six places receive 6, 5, 4, 3, 2 or 1 point. In recent years, only a handful of teams has been capable of winning, yet the last few seasons have been close-fought and Formula One remains as popular as ever.

STAT ATTACK

Recent Formula One Champion Drivers

2011	Sebastian Vettel	Red Bull
2010	Sebastian Vettel	Red Bull
2009	Jenson Button	Brawn
2008	Lewis Hamilton	McLaren
2007	Kimi Räikkönen	Ferrari
2006	Fernando Alonso	Renault
2005	Fernando Alonso	Renault
2004	Michael Schumacher	Ferrari
2003	Michael Schumacher	Ferrari

NASCAR

Founded by Bill France in 1948, NASCAR has risen to become America's favourite motorsport with a live audience measured in millions and an estimated 80 million television spectators during a season.

The Cars

NASCARs for the Sprint Cup are rear-wheel drive beasts with engines capable of generating 800 horsepower, around seven times the amount produced by a family saloon car. They can travel at speeds greater than 320 km/h that on a crowded track can mean some hair-raising heavy racing. The rest of the car is stripped down, according to detailed and strict NASCAR rules with no wing mirrors, a manual four-speed gearbox, a roll cage and other safety features.

MAD //// //// FACT

At the 2003 Carolina Dodge Dealers 400 race, Ricky Craven and Kurt Busch sprinted to the line in the closest finish in NASCAR history. Just two one-thousandths of a second separated the winner, Craven from his rival.

A massed rank of NASCARs enter a turn in the UAW-Ford 500 race. A maximum of 43 cars can qualify for a race. These are held on circuits throughout the United States.

Terry Cook's NASCAR Craftsman Truck catches fire after a crash in the Chevy Silverado HD 250 race at Daytona in 2007.

The Sprint Cup

Known previously as the NEXTEL Cup and Winston Cup, this is the pinnacle of NASCAR and every driver's greatest ambition to win. The competition is 36 races long, each involving intense battles, frequent lead changes and many high-octane thrills and spills in the three to four hours it takes to complete a typical 500-mile (800-kilometre) race.

A race winner nets 185 points, second gets 170 and the points carry all the way down to 43rd and last place, which gains 34 points. Crucial to the standings can be the extra points awarded – an extra five points for any car that leads a lap and a further five points for the driver who leads the most laps in a race. A new innovation from the 2004 season onwards saw the first 26 races count to a ten-race 'Chase for the Championship'.

Other Series

NASCAR organises a number of local and regional series and two further national series. The Nationwide Series is the level below the Sprint Cup and includes old hands and rising stars gaining experience in its 35-race competition that includes events in Canada and Mexico. Souped-up pick-up trucks also get their own competition with the Craftsmen Truck Series. In 1995, Ken Schrader became the first man to win a race in all three national series.

RALLYING AND ENDURANCE

Three of the standout motorsport competitions occur in the classes of rallying and endurance. All push drivers' stamina and the reliability of their vehicles to the limit.

World Rally Championship

The pinnacle of rallying is the World Rally Championship (WRC). It began in 1973 and the 2008 season featured 15 rallies, opening with the historic Monte Carlo Rally that was first held in 1911. Rallies follow throughout Europe as well as in Mexico, Argentina and Japan. Most of the rallies are between 1,000 and 1,800 kilometres long, divided into stages. The top eight finishing cars are awarded points that go to two different championships – one for the driver and the other for the best-competing manufacturer.

The Dakar Rally

The most famous of all off-road competitions, the Dakar Rally, began in 1979. Various routes have been used but nearly all have ended in Dakar, Senegal. Cars, trucks, buggies and bikes all compete in their own groups and classes. Hubert Auriol became the first to win the Dakar in a motorcycle class (1981, 1983) and the car class in 1992 while in 2001, Jutta Kleinschmidt became the first woman to win the Dakar. Fears of terrorist attacks led to the 2008 rally being cancelled and the 2009 race was moved to South America and ran through Argentina and Chile.

Giniel de Villiers takes a turn on his way to victory in the gruelling 2008 Rally dos Sertöes in Brazil

Danish endurance driving legend, Tom Kristensen crosses the finish line to win the 76th edition of the 24 Hours of Le Mans. His 2008 win in an Audi R10 takes his total to eight Le Mans victories.

24 Hours of Le Mans

Considered the ultimate test of sports car endurance, the 24 Hours competition began in 1923. Today, about 50 cars start the race, competing in different classes. Ahead of the three drivers for each car is the ultimate test of stamina and concentration. As many laps of the over 13-kilometre long track have to be completed in the 24 hour period as possible. Racing carries on through the night and into the next day, with drivers contending with all sorts of weather conditions from fog to pouring rain.

Recent Le Mans Winners

2011 Audi R18 TDI
Marcel Fässler, André Lotterer, Benoît Trélvyes

2010 Audi R15 TDI Plus
Mike Rockenfeller, Timo Bernhard, Romain Dumas

2009 Peugeot Sport Total
David Brabham, Marc Gené, Alexander Wurz

2008 Audi R10
Tom Kristensen, Allan McNish, Rinaldo Capello

2007 Audi R10
Frank Biela, Emanuele Pirro, Marco Werner

2006 Audi R10
Frank Biela, Emanuele Pirro, Marco Werner

2005 Audi R8
Tom Kristensen, J. J. Lehto, Marco Werner

2004 Audi R8
Seiji Ara, Tom Kristensen, Rinaldo Capello

2003 Bentley Speed 8
Rinaldo Capello, Tom Kristensen, Guy Smith

MOTORBIKE COMPETITIONS

There are many different competitions for racers on two wheels and even some for three wheels because sidecar racing has its own Superside world championship.

Motocross

The sport of motocross is split into a number of major championships, including the AMA Motocross Championship in America and the FIM World Championship that, despite its name, is held mainly in Europe. Both events feature rounds of races at different motocross tracks and with a massed start of up to 40 riders. With races lasting either 30 or 35 minutes plus a further two laps of the track, the action is intense and crashes or falls are common. This makes Ricky Carmichael's achievement of winning seven championships in a row outstanding.

Motocross legend, Ricky Carmichael soars high in the air during a 2008 X Games competition in California, USA. In both 2002 and 2004, Carmichael notched a perfect season winning all 24 races in the AMA 250cc Outdoor National Motocross Championship.

Who is...

...Valentino Rossi?

Valentino Rossi is the most successful motorcycle racer in the world. A teenage prodigy, Rossi was just 17 in 1996 when he debuted in Grand Prix motorcycle racing. He won the World 125cc Championship the next year. Moving up to bigger bikes and always winning races and championships along the way, Rossi entered the most prestigious competition, MotoGP in 2002 and won the championship not once, but four years in a row. Always sporting the number 46 on his bike, Rossi is known as 'The Doctor' for the clinical way he outsmarts and outraces his opponents.

Valentino Rossi leans into a turn during practise for the 2008 Catalan Grand Prix. Rossi won nine out of the season's 18 races to become 2008 MotoGP world champion.

Grand Prix Racing

Grand Prix motorcycling features purpose-built bikes racing on a series of circuits. In the past, 80cc bikes were the smallest class of machine raced but now, the smallest is 125cc. Above that are 250cc bikes and the top class of riding that for many years featured 500cc bikes. In 2002, these were replaced by 990cc monsters (now 800cc) as the 500cc competition was rebadged MotoGP. A Grand Prix season is made up of around 18 races on circuits throughout the world including Assen, Le Mans and Indianapolis. First place receives 25 points, second place 20, third place 16 and fourth place 13. The points then go down a point per position from 11 points for fifth place to one point for fifteenth.

Superbike World Championship

World Superbikes feature production motorcycles that are specially tuned and equipped to race according to strict rules. They are much cheaper than the one-off MotoGP machines, but barely slower. The World Championship began in 1988 and now features about 14 rounds. Each round consists of two races at the same circuit. It uses the same points-scoring system as MotoGP but for each race meaning a double winner on a weekend scoops 50 points.

STAT ATTACK

World Superbike Winners

2007 James Toseland (Honda)

2006 Troy Bayliss (Ducati)

2005 Troy Corser (Suzuki)

2004 James Toseland (Ducati)

2003 Neil Hodgson (Ducati)

2002 Colin Edwards (Honda)

LEGENDS

Motorsports have generated dozens of truly great drivers and riders who showed bravery, skill, timing and nerve to capture races and titles. Here are six of the very best.

Juan Manuel Fangio

The awesome Argentinean was 39 years old when the Formula One World Championship began in 1950. But, despite being of an age when most racing drivers had retired, he demonstrated his courage and racing brilliance over the next seven years. Despite breaking his neck and missing much of the 1952 season, Fangio dominated with 24 wins out of 51 Grand Prix. He won the World Championship in 1951, came second in 1953 and then won four in a row (1954–1957).

Richard Petty

The 'King' (right) was NASCAR's most successful driver winning 200 races over a 32-year career. Only one other driver, Dave Pearson, has won more than 100. A marvellous racer and highly popular with fans, Petty also managed a truly staggering 550 top-five finishes in NASCAR racing. Although he retired from racing in 1992, the Petty name is still at the forefront of American motorsports with his own successful NASCAR team and his son, Kyle a prominent driver.

Ayrton Senna

Considered by many to be the most natural racer in Formula One history, Brazilian Ayrton Senna began his racing career in karting and then won the British Formula Three Championship in 1983. After serving an apprenticeship in Formula One with the Toleman and Lotus teams, Senna moved to McLaren where he won three World Championships. His glittering Formula One career, with 65 pole positions and 41 race wins, was tragically cut short with his death from a crash at Imola in 1994.

Tommi Makinen

Controlled yet aggressive and fearless, Makinen (left) began farm tractor racing before starting car rallying in the mid-1980s. The Finn established Mitsubishi's Ralliart team as a major force in the 1990s with an impressive series of rally wins that saw him become the first driver to win the World Rally Championship four times in a row (1996, 1997, 1998 and 1999). He also finished third in a fifth championship and later moved to Subaru, before retiring at the end of 2003.

Giacomo Agostini

The great Italian motorcyclist won an incredible 122 motorcycle Grand Prix races during the 1960s and 1970s to make him the most successful ever. Between 1968 and 1974 he won every 350cc World Championships and, if that was not enough, Agostini also scooped eight 500cc World Championships between 1966 and 1975. He also won 10 TT races out of the 16 that he entered. After retiring at the end of 1977, he became boss of the Yamaha race team.

Stephan Peterhansel

The ultimate off-road racer, Frenchman Stephan Peterhansel started out as a Motocross rider who later graduated to endurance rallies. He won six out of seven Paris-Dakar Rally titles (now the Dakar Rally) for motorcycles between 1991 and 1998 but in 1999, he changed over to four wheels, winning the Paris-Dakar Rally for cars in 2004, 2005, 2006 and the Dakar Rally 2012.

GLOSSARY

Aerodynamics The science of how air flows around a race vehicle as it moves.

Apex The part of a corner where the car runs closest to the edge of the track.

Capacity One way of measuring the size of the engine, usually given as cubic centimetres (cc). The lower the cc, the smaller the engine.

Chicane A pair of turns on a track going one way and then the other, mostly placed along a straight to slow cars and bikes down.

Cockpit The space in a car for the driver and the controls.

Downforce A powerful force caused by the way air flows around a car that helps push the car down onto the track or ground.

G-force A way of measuring the force of gravity on a vehicle and racer when the vehicle is speeding up, slowing down sharply or turning a tight corner. For example, 4G is a force compared to four times the force of gravity.

Hairpin A roughly 180 degree corner that drivers and riders have to slow down greatly to negotiate.

Handling How a car responds when racing, particularly to changes in direction and different speeds.

Lapped When a race vehicle has completed at least one whole lap less than other vehicles.

Open wheel Types of racing cars, usually single-seater vehicles, with their wheels outside of their bodies.

Pit crew The team of engineers and mechanics who works on vehicles when they come into the pit lane.

Pit lane The road that runs from the edge of the track to the teams' garages where a vehicle can travel to re-fuel and make repairs during a pit stop.

Pole position The best position on the front of a starting grid given to the car or bike that qualifies with the fastest time.

Production car/motorbikes A vehicle that is produced in a factory for sale to the public.

Qualifying Races or timed sessions that decide the order of the starting grid at the beginning of a race.

Rolling start A start of a race that already sees the cars on the move before the starting signal is given.

Rookie A driver or rider who is new to the sport.

Slick A type of tyre with no tread used to obtain maximum grip.

Standing start Starting a race from a stationary or still position.

Starting grid The area of the track where the cars line up just before a race starts.

Suspension The system of springs, shock absorbers and other parts that are joined to the wheels or axles.

Tactics The ways a driver or rider and his team decide to run a race.

Telemetry Data about the race vehicle sent to the team's headquarters by radio signals.

WEBSITES

WWW.FORMULA1.COM

Formula One's official website is full of interesting in-depth features on the drivers, teams, the technology and great guides to the race circuits.

WWW.NASCAR.COM

The official NASCAR racing website contains lots of interesting facts, statistics and news on races, drivers and team bosses.

WWW.WRC.COM

This is the website to head for information on the World Rally Championships. It comes complete with lots of photos, video clips and race news and interviews.

WWW.AUTORACING1.COM

A busy and frequently updated motorsports news website with the latest on IndyCars, Formula One and NASCAR amongst other classes.

WWW.MOTOGP.COM

The official MotoGP website contains all the latest on the races of the season.

WWW.ETRACKSONLINE.CO.UK

A huge database of motorsports tracks of the world searchable by name and country.

Note to parents and teachers:

Every effort has been made by the publishers to ensure that these websites are suitable for children, that they are of the highest educational value, and that they contain no inappropriate or offensive material. However, because of the nature of the Internet, it is impossible to guarantee that the contents of these sites will not be altered. We strongly advise that Internet access is supervised by a responsible adult.

INDEX